Poke
cakes

Printed in the United States of America
by G&R Publishing Co.

Distributed By:

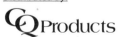Products

507 Industrial Street
Waverly, IA 50677

ISBN-13: 978-1-56383-481-3
ISBN-10: 1-56383-481-2
Item #7080

Poke Cakes
Sweet Simplicity

1
Poke It

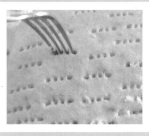

2
Fill It

3
Frost It

Poke Cake

Tuxedo

Ingredients

1 (15.25 oz.) box white cake mix

Egg whites, oil, and water as directed on cake mix box

2 T. unsweetened cocoa powder

¼ C. hot fudge ice cream topping

2 (3.3 oz.) boxes white chocolate instant pudding mix

4 C. milk

1 (8 oz.) tub whipped topping, thawed

Chocolate and white chocolate chips

Directions

1 Preheat oven to 350°. Spray a 9 x 13″ baking pan with cooking spray.

2 Follow directions on cake mix box to prepare cake batter. Transfer ⅓ of batter to a separate bowl and stir in cocoa powder. Spread remaining white batter in prepared pan and drop chocolate batter on top by spoonfuls. Drag a knife through batters until swirled together. Bake for 35 minutes or until cake tests done. Let cool for 15 minutes.

3 With the handle of a wooden spoon, poke holes in warm cake at 1″ intervals.

4 Warm the fudge topping slightly and drizzle over cake and into holes.

5 In a large bowl, whisk together both pudding mixes and milk until smooth and mixture just begins to thicken. Slowly pour pudding mixture over cake, allowing it to fill holes and coat cake. Refrigerate for 3 hours.

6 Frost with whipped topping and sprinkle with chips.

Patriotic Poke

Ingredients

1 (16.25 oz.) box white
cake mix

Egg whites, oil, and
water as directed
on cake mix box

1 (3 oz.) box berry blue
gelatin

1 (3 oz.) box strawberry
gelatin

White Baker's Frosting
(recipe follows)

Red, white, and blue
sprinkles

Directions

1. Preheat oven to 350°. Line 12 jumbo muffin cups with paper liners.

2. Follow directions on cake mix box to prepare cake batter; divide it evenly among prepared muffin cups. Bake for 25 minutes or until cupcakes test done. Remove cupcakes to a wire rack set over a rimmed baking sheet and let cool for 15 minutes.

3. With a fork, poke holes in warm cupcakes, about ½″ apart.

4. Combine berry blue gelatin with 1 cup boiling water and stir until dissolved. Stir in ½ cup cold water. In the same way, dissolve strawberry gelatin.

5. Spoon about half the blue gelatin mixture over six cupcakes to fill holes. Spoon half the red gelatin mixture over remaining six cupcakes. (Reserve extra gelatin for another use.) Refrigerate cupcakes for 3 hours.

6. Cut cupcakes in half crosswise. Spread White Baker's Frosting on cut side of cupcake bottoms. Set opposite color cupcake top on frosting, like a layer cake. Frost cupcakes and decorate with sprinkles.

White Baker's Frosting

Beat together ½ C. white vegetable shortening, ¼ C. hot water, ¼ tsp. salt, 1 tsp. clear vanilla extract, ½ tsp. butter flavoring, and about 4 C. powdered sugar until light and fluffy.

Banana Cream

Ingredients

1 (15.25 oz.) box yellow cake mix

Eggs, oil, and water as directed on cake mix box

2 (3.4 oz.) boxes banana instant pudding mix

4 C. milk

1 (8 oz.) tub whipped topping, thawed

Graham cracker crumbs

Sliced bananas

Directions

1. Follow directions on cake mix box to prepare and bake a 9 x 13″ cake. Let cool for 5 minutes.

2. With the handle of a wooden spoon, poke holes in warm cake, about 1″ apart.

3. Whisk together both pudding mixes and milk until smooth and mixture just begins to thicken. Slowly pour pudding mixture over cake and spread to fill holes and coat cake. Refrigerate for 2 hours.

4. Spread whipped topping over pudding layer and refrigerate. Before serving, sprinkle with graham cracker crumbs and top with banana slices.

Orange Delight

Ingredients

1 (15.25 oz.) box French Vanilla cake mix

Eggs and oil as directed on cake mix box

1 C. orange juice (use in place of water listed on box)

½ tsp. orange flavoring

1 (3 oz.) box orange gelatin

Orange Buttercream *(recipe follows)*

Directions

1 Preheat oven to 350°. Spray two 9″ round cake pans with cooking spray.

2 In a large mixing bowl, combine cake mix, eggs, oil, and orange juice; beat as directed on cake mix box. Stir in orange flavoring. Divide batter evenly among prepared pans and bake for recommended time or until cakes test done. Let cool completely in pans.

3 With a fork, poke holes in each cake at ½″ intervals.

4 Combine gelatin with 1 cup boiling water and stir until completely dissolved; let cool slightly. Slowly pour half the mixture over each cake, allowing it to fill holes. Refrigerate at least 2 hours.

5 Carefully remove one cake from pan and set on a serving plate, rounded side up. Trim off top of cake, making it level. Spread about ¼ of the Orange Buttercream over cake layer to within ½″ of edges. Place second cake layer on top; frost sides and top of layer cake with remaining frosting. Refrigerate until serving time.

Orange Buttercream

Beat together 6 oz. softened cream cheese and ¼ C. softened butter until creamy. Add 1 tsp. orange flavoring. Gradually beat in 5 C. powdered sugar until smooth and fluffy. Stir in orange gel food coloring to desired shade.

note Can be made in a 9 x 13″ pan, too.

Peanut Butter Chocolate

Ingredients

1 (15.25 oz.) box devil's
food cake mix

Eggs, oil, and water
as directed on cake
mix box

1 (14 oz.) can sweetened
condensed milk

1 (12.8 oz.) jar hot fudge
ice cream topping

¼ C. creamy peanut butter

Peanut Butter Topping
(recipe follows)

Directions

1 Preheat oven to 350°. Spray 12 ramekins or oven-safe custard cups with cooking spray.

2 Follow directions on cake mix box to prepare cake batter and divide it evenly among prepared ramekins. Bake for 20 to 25 minutes or until cakes test done. Let cool completely.

3 With the handle of a wooden spoon, poke holes in each cake at ½˝ to 1˝ intervals.

4 Slowly pour sweetened condensed milk over cakes, allowing it to fill holes and coat cakes.

5 In a microwave-safe bowl, combine fudge topping and peanut butter; microwave for 30 seconds. Stir until smooth and spread over cakes.

6 Frost cakes with Peanut Butter Topping and refrigerate at least 4 hours or overnight. Before serving, sprinkle with chopped peanut butter cups or Reese's Pieces, if desired.

Peanut Butter Topping

In a large bowl, whisk together 3 T. creamy peanut butter and 1 (8 oz.) tub thawed whipped topping until well blended.

note Can be made in a 9 x 13˝ pan, too.

Black Cherry-
White Chocolate

Ingredients

1 (16.5 oz.) box white cake mix

Egg whites, oil, and water as directed on cake mix box

1 (3 oz.) box black cherry gelatin

White Chocolate Topping *(recipe follows)*

Directions

1 Follow directions on cake mix box to prepare and bake a 9 x 13″ cake. Let cool for 15 minutes.

2 With a fork, poke holes in warm cake at 1″ intervals.

3 Combine gelatin with 1 cup boiling water and stir until completely dissolved. Stir in ¾ cup cold water. Slowly pour mixture over cake, allowing it to fill holes. Refrigerate for 3 hours.

4 Frost cake with White Chocolate Topping and refrigerate. Before serving, top with pitted cherries or cherry sauce and white chocolate, if desired.

White Chocolate Topping

Whisk together 1 (3.3 oz.) box white chocolate instant pudding mix and 1 C. milk until smooth. Stir in 1 (8 oz.) tub thawed whipped topping.

Aloha Pineapple

Ingredients

1 (20 oz.) can crushed pineapple in juice

1 (15.25 oz.) box yellow cake mix

Eggs and oil as directed on cake mix box

1 (8 oz.) pkg. cream cheese, softened

1 (3.4 oz.) box vanilla instant pudding mix

1½ C. milk

2 C. whipped topping, thawed

Directions

1 Preheat oven to 350°. Spray a 9 x 13˝ baking pan with cooking spray.

2 Drain pineapple and reserve the juice. Add enough water to juice to equal amount of water listed on cake mix box; set aside.

3 In a large mixing bowl, combine cake mix, eggs, oil, and water/juice mixture; beat as directed on box. Spread batter in prepared pan and bake for recommended time or until cake tests done. Let cool completely.

4 With the handle of a wooden spoon, poke holes in cake at 1˝ intervals.

5 Spread pineapple over cake, pressing down gently to fill holes.

6 In a medium mixing bowl, beat together cream cheese, pudding mix, and milk until smooth. Spread over pineapple layer.

7 Frost with whipped topping and refrigerate. Before serving, sprinkle with toasted coconut,* if desired.

*Toasted Coconut

Place coconut in a single layer on a baking sheet. Bake at 350° for 5 to 8 minutes or until golden brown.

Cookies & Cream

Ingredients

1 (15.25 oz.) box chocolate cake mix

Eggs, oil, and water as directed on cake mix box

2 (4.2 oz.) boxes Oreo Cookies 'n Creme instant pudding mix

4 C. milk

Crushed Oreos

Directions

1 Follow directions on cake mix box to prepare and bake a 9 x 13˝ cake. Let cool for 15 minutes.

2 With the handle of a wooden spoon, poke holes in warm cake, about 1˝ apart.

3 Stir together both boxes of pudding mix and milk until just blended. Slowly pour half the mixture over cake, allowing it to fill holes and coat cake. Let stand for 15 minutes and then spread remaining pudding mixture over the top. Refrigerate for 3 hours.

4 Just before serving, sprinkle with crushed Oreos.

Raspberry Lemonade

Ingredients

1 (3 oz.) box raspberry gelatin

1 (16.25 oz.) box white cake mix

½ C. frozen lemonade concentrate, thawed, divided

⅓ C. vegetable oil

4 egg whites

Vanilla Whip
(recipe follows)

Serves 24

Directions

1 Preheat oven to 350°. Line 24 muffin cups with paper liners.

2 Combine gelatin with 1 cup boiling water and stir until completely dissolved.

3 In a large mixing bowl, combine cake mix, ¼ cup gelatin mixture, ¼ cup lemonade concentrate, oil, egg whites, and ¼ cup cold water; beat as directed on cake mix box. Divide batter among prepared muffin cups and bake cupcakes for recommended time or until they test done. Remove cupcakes to a wire rack set over a rimmed baking sheet and let cool slightly.

4 With a fork, poke holes in warm cupcakes at ½" intervals.

5 Stir together remaining gelatin mixture and lemonade concentrate. Slowly pour mixture over cupcakes, allowing it to fill holes. Refrigerate for 1 hour.

6 Frost cupcakes with Vanilla Whip and garnish with fresh raspberries and lemon zest, if desired.

Vanilla Whip

Stir together 1 (12 oz.) tub whipped vanilla frosting and 1 C. thawed whipped topping.

Pumpkin Caramel

Ingredients

- 1 (16.5 oz.) box yellow cake mix
- 1 C. pumpkin (from a 15 oz. can)
- ⅓ C. vegetable oil
- 4 eggs
- 2 tsp. pumpkin pie spice
- 1 (14 oz.) can sweetened condensed milk
- 1 (12.25 oz.) jar caramel ice cream topping
- Butterscotch-Caramel Buttercream *(recipe follows)*
- Chopped pecans

Directions

1 Preheat oven to 350°. Spray a 9 x 13" baking pan with cooking spray.

2 In a large mixing bowl, combine cake mix, pumpkin, oil, eggs, pumpkin pie spice, and ⅓ cup water; beat as directed on cake mix box. Spread batter in prepared pan and bake for recommended time or until cake tests done.

3 With the handle of a wooden spoon, poke holes in hot cake at ½" to 1" intervals.

4 Slowly pour sweetened condensed milk over cake, allowing it to fill holes and coat cake.

5 Heat caramel topping and pour evenly over cake. Run a knife around sides of pan to loosen cake. Cool for 30 minutes and then refrigerate for 2 hours.

6 Frost with Butterscotch-Caramel Buttercream and sprinkle with pecans.

Butterscotch-Caramel Buttercream

Cream together 6 T. softened butter, 6 T. butterscotch-caramel ice cream topping, ¾ tsp. vanilla extract, and a pinch of salt. Gradually beat in 3 C. powdered sugar alternately with 1½ to 2 T. milk until blended and smooth.

Mocktail Margarita

Ingredients

- 1 (16.25 oz.) box white cake mix
- ¾ C. plus ⅓ C. nonalcoholic margarita mix, divided
- ⅓ C. vegetable oil
- 1 T. lime zest
- 3 egg whites
- 1 (7 oz.) container marshmallow creme
- 1 (5 oz.) can evaporated milk
- 1 (8 oz.) tub whipped topping, thawed
- 1½ C. crushed pretzels
- ½ C. sugar
- ½ C. butter, melted

Directions

1. Preheat oven to 350°. Spray a 9 x 13" baking pan with cooking spray.

2. In a large mixing bowl, combine cake mix, ¾ cup margarita mix, oil, lime zest, egg whites, and ½ cup water; beat as directed on cake mix box. Spread batter in prepared pan and bake for 35 to 45 minutes or until cake tests done. Let cool for 15 minutes.

3. With a meat fork, poke holes in warm cake at ½" intervals.

4. In a medium saucepan over low heat, combine marshmallow creme and evaporated milk, whisking until melted and smooth. Remove from heat and stir in remaining ⅓ cup margarita mix; let set for 5 minutes. Slowly pour mixture over cake, allowing it to fill holes and coat cake. Cool completely.

5. Frost with whipped topping.

6. In a medium bowl, stir together pretzels, sugar, and butter; sprinkle over whipped topping before serving. Garnish with fresh lime slices or lime zest, if desired.

Chocolate Peppermint

Ingredients

1 (16.5 oz.) box devil's food cake mix

Eggs, oil, and water as directed on cake mix box

½ C. peppermint-flavored liquid coffee creamer

1 (14 oz.) can sweetened condensed milk

¼ tsp. peppermint extract

Chocolate-Peppermint Frosting *(recipe follows)*

Directions

1 Follow directions on cake mix box to prepare and bake a 9 x 13″ cake. Let cool for 15 minutes.

2 With the handle of a wooden spoon, poke holes in warm cake, about 1″ apart.

3 In a large spouted measuring cup, whisk together coffee creamer, sweetened condensed milk, and peppermint extract. Slowly pour mixture over cake, allowing it to fill holes and coat cake. Refrigerate for 2 hours.

4 Frost cake with Chocolate-Peppermint Frosting. Before serving, sprinkle with coarsely chopped peppermint patties, if desired.

Chocolate-Peppermint Frosting

Stir together 1 (16 oz.) tub chocolate frosting and ½ teaspoon peppermint extract.

Coconut Lime

Ingredients

1 (15.25 oz.) box white cake mix

Eggs, oil, and water as directed on cake mix box

½ C. sweetened flaked coconut

1 (3 oz.) box lime gelatin

1 (13.5 oz.) can coconut milk, chilled overnight

1 C. powdered sugar

½ to 1 C. toasted coconut*

Directions

1 Follow directions on cake mix box to prepare a 9 x 13″ cake, stirring ½ cup coconut into batter before baking. Bake for recommended time or until cake tests done. Let cool completely.

2 With a fork, poke holes in cake at 1″ intervals.

3 Combine gelatin with 1 cup boiling water and stir until completely dissolved. Stir in ½ cup cold water. Slowly pour mixture over cake, allowing it to fill holes. Refrigerate for 1 hour.

4 Without shaking can, open coconut milk. With a spoon, carefully transfer opaque white foam from can to a medium bowl, reserving the clear syrup in the bottom of the can.

5 Whip foam in bowl on high speed for 4 minutes or until soft peaks form. Add powdered sugar and 1 tablespoon syrup from can. Beat until well blended. Refrigerate for 15 minutes and then spread mixture over cake. Sprinkle with toasted coconut and chill until serving time.

*Toasted Coconut

Place coconut in a single layer on a baking sheet. Bake at 350° for 5 to 8 minutes or until golden brown.

Cappuccino Hazelnut

Ingredients

1 (15.25 oz.) golden vanilla cake mix

Eggs, oil, and water as directed on cake mix box

1 to 2 C. chopped toasted hazelnuts or filberts*

¼ C. brewed coffee

Dark Chocolate Ganache
(recipe follows)

Vanilla Frosting
(recipe follows)

Directions

1 Follow directions on cake mix box to prepare a 9 x 13" cake, stirring 1 cup hazelnuts into batter before baking, if desired. Bake for recommended time or until cake tests done.

2 With a meat fork, poke holes in hot cake, about 1" apart.

3 Slowly drizzle coffee over cake and into holes. Cool completely.

4 Frost with Dark Chocolate Ganache and sprinkle with 1 cup toasted hazelnuts. Pipe Vanilla Frosting over the top.

Dark Chocolate Ganache

Heat 1 C. whipping cream to simmering. Remove from heat; add 4 oz. chopped bittersweet chocolate and ¼ C. dark chocolate chips, stirring until melted. Cool completely. Transfer to a bowl and beat until just thickened and spreading consistency (do not over-beat).

Vanilla Frosting

Stir together 2 T. softened butter and 2 T. vegetable shortening. Gradually beat in 1 C. powdered sugar and 1 to 2 T. milk until thick and smooth.

*Toasted Hazelnuts

Place hazelnuts in a single layer on a baking sheet. Bake at 350° for 8 to 10 minutes or until golden.

Root Beer Float

Ingredients

- 1 (15.25 oz.) box yellow cake mix
- 1 (20 oz.) bottle root beer, divided
- ¼ C. vegetable oil

- 3 eggs
- ½ C. powdered sugar
- Ice cream
- Root Beer Frosting, optional *(recipe follows)*

Directions

1 Preheat oven to 350°. Line 24 muffin cups with paper liners.

2 In a large mixing bowl, beat together cake mix, 1½ cups root beer, oil, and eggs on medium speed until smooth and well blended. Divide mixture evenly among prepared muffin cups and bake for recommended time or until cupcakes test done. Remove cupcakes to a wire rack set over a rimmed baking sheet and let cool for 15 minutes.

3 With a fork, poke holes in warm cupcakes, about ½″ apart.

4 In a spouted bowl, mix powdered sugar and 3 tablespoons root beer until smooth. Drizzle mixture over cupcakes to fill holes. Serve with ice cream or frost with Root Beer Frosting, if desired.

Root Beer Frosting

Cream together ½ C. softened butter and ½ tsp. root beer concentrate. Gradually beat in 3¾ C. powdered sugar alternately with ¼ C. milk until smooth.

Boston Cream

Ingredients

1 (16.5 oz.) box yellow cake mix

Eggs, oil, and water as directed on cake mix box

2 (3.4 oz.) boxes French vanilla instant pudding mix, divided

4 C. milk, divided

Chocolate Icing *(recipe follows)*

Directions

1. Follow directions on cake mix box to prepare and bake a 9 x 13″ cake. Let cool for 15 minutes.

2. With the handle of a wooden spoon, poke holes in warm cake about 1″ apart.

3. Whisk together one box pudding mix and 2 cups milk until smooth but still thin. Slowly pour mixture over cake, allowing it to fill holes and coat cake. Refrigerate for 1 hour.

4. Whisk together remaining box of pudding mix with remaining 2 cups milk until mixture just begins to thicken. Pour pudding mixture over cake and spread evenly (you may not use all of it). Chill for 2 hours.

5. Prepare Chocolate Icing and spread immediately over cake. Refrigerate until set. If desired, top with whipped cream and fresh berries before serving.

Chocolate Icing

In a saucepan over low heat, melt ¼ C. butter and 2 oz. chopped unsweetened chocolate, stirring constantly. Let cool for 4 minutes. Beat in 2 C. powdered sugar, ¼ C. boiling water, and 1 tsp. vanilla extract until smooth.

Cherry Limeade

Ingredients

1 (16.5 oz.) box white cake mix

1¼ C. lemon-lime soda

⅓ C. vegetable oil

3 egg whites

2 tsp. lime zest

1 (3 oz.) box cherry gelatin

Lime Buttercream
(recipe follows)

Directions

1 Preheat oven to 350°. Grease and flour two 9 x 9″ baking pans.

2 In a large mixing bowl, combine cake mix, soda, oil, egg whites, and lime zest; beat as directed on cake mix box. Divide batter evenly among prepared pans and bake for 27 to 31 minutes or until cakes test done. Cool cakes in pans for 20 minutes.

3 With a fork, poke holes in warm cakes at ½″ intervals.

4 Combine gelatin with 1 cup boiling water and stir until completely dissolved; cool slightly. Slowly pour half the mixture over each cake, allowing it to fill holes. Refrigerate for 2 hours.

5 Carefully remove one cake from pan and set on a serving plate, rounded side up. Trim off top of cake, making it level. Spread cake with half the Lime Buttercream to within ½″ of edges and place the other cake layer on top. Frost with remaining buttercream and garnish with lime zest, if desired.

Lime Buttercream

Cream together ½ C. softened butter, 2 tsp. lime zest, 1 tsp. vanilla extract, and ⅛ tsp. salt. Gradually beat in 4¼ C. powdered sugar alternately with 3 T. lime juice and 1 T. milk until blended and smooth. Stir in green gel food coloring to desired shade.

note Can be made in a 9 x 13″ pan, too.

Black Forest

Ingredients

1 (15.25 oz.) box chocolate cake mix

Eggs, oil, and water as directed on cake mix box

1 (3 oz.) box cherry gelatin

1 (21 oz.) can cherry pie filling

1 (16 oz.) tub whipped topping, thawed

Directions

1. Follow directions on cake mix box to prepare and bake a 9 x 13" cake.

2. With the handle of a wooden spoon, poke holes in hot cake at 1" intervals. Let cool for 15 minutes.

3. Combine gelatin with 1 cup boiling water and stir until completely dissolved; let cool slightly. Slowly pour mixture over cake, allowing it to fill holes. Refrigerate at least 1 hour.

4. Just before serving, top cake with pie filling and whipped topping. Garnish with chocolate shavings, if desired.

French Toast

Ingredients

- 1 (15.25 oz.) box French vanilla cake mix

- ½ tsp. plus ⅛ tsp. ground nutmeg, divided

- 2¼ tsp. ground cinnamon, divided

- 3 eggs plus 1 egg yolk

- ⅓ C. melted butter, cooled

- 3 C. milk, divided

- ¼ C. sour cream

- 1 T. vanilla extract

- 3 T. plus ¼ C. pure maple syrup

- 1 (3.4 oz.) box vanilla instant pudding mix

- Sweetened Whipped Cream *(recipe follows)*

Directions

1 Preheat oven to 350°. Grease and flour a 9 x 13˝ baking pan.

2 In a large mixing bowl, combine cake mix, ½ teaspoon nutmeg and 2 teaspoons cinnamon. Add eggs and egg yolk; beat well. Add butter, 1 cup milk, and sour cream; beat until well blended. Mix in vanilla and 3 tablespoons syrup. Spread batter in prepared pan and bake for 28 to 33 minutes or until cake tests done. Let cool for 15 minutes.

3 With the handle of a wooden spoon, poke holes in warm cake, about 1˝ apart.

4 Slowly drizzle remaining ¼ cup syrup over cake and into holes.

5 In a separate bowl, whisk together pudding mix with remaining ⅛ teaspoon nutmeg, ¼ teaspoon cinnamon, and 2 cups milk until smooth but still thin. Slowly pour mixture over cake, allowing it to fill holes and coat cake. Refrigerate at least 1 hour.

6 Just before serving, spread Sweetened Whipped Cream over cake and sprinkle lightly with nutmeg or cinnamon, if desired.

Sweetened Whipped Cream

In a chilled deep mixing bowl with chilled beaters, beat 1 C. whipping cream until frothy. Gradually beat in 2 to 3 tablespoons sugar until soft peaks form. Don't over-beat.

Double Lemon

Ingredients

1 (15.25 oz.) box white cake mix

Egg whites, oil, and water as directed on cake mix box

1 (6 oz.) box lemon gelatin

1 (22 oz.) can lemon pie filling

1 (8 oz.) tub whipped topping, thawed

Directions

1 Follow directions on cake mix box to prepare and bake two 9" round cake layers. Let cool completely in pans.

2 With a fork, poke holes in cakes at ½" intervals.

3 Combine gelatin with 2 cups boiling water and stir until completely dissolved; let cool slightly. Slowly pour half the mixture over each cake, allowing it to fill holes. Refrigerate at least 3 hours.

4 Carefully remove one cake from pan and set on a serving plate, rounded side up. Trim off top of cake, making it level. Spread half the pie filling over cake layer to within ½" of edges. Place second cake layer on top and spread with remaining pie filling.

5 Frost sides and top of layer cake with whipped topping. Serve promptly or refrigerate for up to 3 hours. If desired, garnish with strips of fresh lemon peel.

note Can be made in a 9 x 13" pan, too.

Cinnamon Roll

Ingredients

1 (15.25 oz.) box yellow cake mix

4 eggs

1 C. sour cream

¾ C. vegetable oil

1 C. butter, softened

1 C. brown sugar

2 T. flour

1 T. ground cinnamon

2 C. powdered sugar

5 T. milk

1 tsp. vanilla extract

Directions

1 Preheat oven to 350°. Spray the bottom of a 9 x 13″ baking pan with cooking spray.

2 In a large mixing bowl, combine cake mix, eggs, sour cream, and oil; beat as directed on cake mix box. Spread batter in prepared pan and set aside.

3 In a small bowl, beat together butter, brown sugar, flour, and cinnamon until smooth and creamy. Drop cinnamon filling onto cake batter by spoonfuls. Drag a knife through batter and filling until swirled together. Bake for 33 to 40 minutes or until cake tests done. Let cool for 15 minutes.

4 With a fork, poke holes in warm cake 1″ to 2″ apart.

5 In a spouted bowl, whisk together powdered sugar, milk, and vanilla until smooth. Drizzle mixture over cake, allowing it to fill holes and swirls. Serve warm or at room temperature.

note Refrigerate cake
for easy slicing.

Strawberry Rhubarb

Ingredients

1½ C. sugar, divided

½ C. butter, softened

4 large egg yolks, beaten

1 C. milk

1½ tsp. vanilla extract

2 C. flour

2 tsp. baking powder

½ tsp. salt

3 C. chopped fresh or frozen rhubarb

1 (3 oz.) box strawberry gelatin

1 (10.6 oz.) tub Cool Whip brand Cream Cheese Frosting, thawed

Directions

1 Preheat oven to 350°. Grease and flour a 9 x 13˝ baking pan.

2 In a large mixing bowl, beat together 1 cup sugar and butter until creamy. Add egg yolks and beat well. Beat in milk and vanilla. Add flour, baking powder, and salt; mix until well blended. Set aside.

3 Arrange rhubarb over bottom of prepared pan; sprinkle with remaining ½ cup sugar. Pour cake batter evenly over rhubarb and bake for 35 to 40 minutes or until cake tests done. Let cool completely.

4 With a fork, poke holes in cake at 1˝ intervals.

5 Combine gelatin with 1 cup boiling water and stir until completely dissolved. Stir in ½ cup cold water. Slowly pour mixture over cake, allowing it to fill holes. Refrigerate for 3 hours or overnight.

6 Spread Cool Whip Frosting over cake and refrigerate. Just before serving, garnish with fresh strawberries, if desired.

Classic Carrot

Ingredients

1 (15.25 oz.) box carrot cake mix

Eggs, oil, and water as directed on cake mix box

1 (14 oz.) can sweetened condensed milk

1 C. whipped topping, thawed

1 (10.6 oz.) tub Cool Whip brand Cream Cheese Frosting, thawed

¼ C. caramel ice cream topping

½ C. chopped pecans

Directions

1 Follow directions on cake mix box to prepare and bake a 9 x 13″ cake. Let cool completely.

2 With the handle of a wooden spoon, poke holes in cake at 1″ intervals.

3 Slowly pour sweetened condensed milk over cake, allowing it to fill holes and coat cake.

4 In a medium bowl, stir together whipped topping and Cool Whip Frosting. Spread evenly over cake.

5 Drizzle caramel topping over frosting and sprinkle with pecans. Refrigerate at least 4 hours.

Butterfinger

Ingredients

1 (18.25 oz.) box marble
cake mix

Eggs, oil, and water
as directed on cake
mix box

1 (14 oz.) can sweetened
condensed milk

¾ C. caramel ice cream
topping

Sour Cream Chocolate
Frosting *(recipe follows)*

6 snack-size Butterfinger
candy bars, coarsely
crushed

1 square white almond
bark, melted

Directions

1 Preheat oven to 350°. Spray six 3¾ x 5⁵⁄₁₆″ foil loaf pans* with cooking spray.

2 Follow directions on cake mix box to prepare cake batter; divide it evenly among prepared pans, swirling batter as directed. Bake for 20 to 25 minutes or until cakes test done. Let cool for 10 minutes.

3 With a fork, poke holes in warm cakes at 1″ intervals.

4 In a large spouted measuring cup, mix sweetened condensed milk and caramel topping. Slowly pour mixture over cake, allowing it to fill holes and coat cake. Refrigerate until completely cool.

5 Frost cakes with Sour Cream Chocolate Frosting. Sprinkle with crushed candy bars and drizzle melted bark over the top.

* For easy gift-giving, cover with plastic wrap and add a bow.

Sour Cream Chocolate Frosting

In a saucepan over medium heat, melt ¾ C. milk chocolate chips, ¼ C. semi-sweet chocolate chips, and ¼ C. butter, stirring often. Let cool for 5 minutes. Stir in 2 T. sour cream, a dash of salt, and 1 teaspoon vanilla extract. Beat in 2 C. powdered sugar until light and fluffy. Spread promptly.

note Can be made in a 9 x 13″ pan, too.

Kool Blue

Ingredients

1 (16.5 oz.) box white cake mix

Eggs, oil, and water as directed on cake mix box

1 C. sugar

1 (.22 oz.) pkg. blue raspberry-lemonade unsweetened soft drink mix

Kool-Blue Frosting *(recipe follows)*

Directions

1 Follow directions on cake mix box to prepare and bake 24 cupcakes. Remove cupcakes to a wire rack set over a rimmed baking sheet; cool completely.

2 In a small saucepan over medium-high heat, heat sugar, drink mix, and 1 cup water to boiling, stirring until dissolved. Set aside to cool.

3 With a fork, poke holes in cupcakes, about ½″ apart.

4 Slowly pour cooled sugar mixture over cupcakes, allowing it to fill holes.

5 Frost with Kool-Blue Frosting and sprinkle with colored sugar and/or decorating sprinkles, if desired.

Kool-Blue Frosting

Stir together 2 (12 oz.) tubs whipped white frosting and 1 (.22 oz.) pkg. blue raspberry-lemonade unsweetened soft drink mix until well blended.

Peanut Butter Bliss

Ingredients

- ½ C. plus ⅓ C. creamy peanut butter, divided
- ¾ C. butter, softened, divided
- 4 eggs
- 1 (15.25 oz.) box butter cake mix

- ¼ C. milk
- ½ C. powdered sugar
- 2 tsp. vanilla extract
- Peanut Butter Frosting *(recipe follows)*

Directions

1 Preheat oven to 325°. Spray the bottom of a 9 x 13″ baking pan with cooking spray.

2 In a large mixing bowl, beat together ½ cup peanut butter and ½ cup butter until creamy. Beat in eggs, one at a time. Alternately add cake mix and ⅔ cup water, mixing well after each addition. Spread batter in prepared pan and bake for 30 to 35 minutes or until cake tests done. Let cool for 10 minutes.

3 With the handle of a wooden spoon, poke holes in warm cake, about 1″ apart.

4 In a small saucepan over medium-low heat, combine remaining ⅓ cup peanut butter, remaining ¼ cup butter, and milk; cook and stir until mixture comes to a boil. Remove from heat and whisk in powdered sugar and vanilla. Spread immediately over cake, allowing mixture to fill holes and coat cake.

5 Frost cake with Peanut Butter Frosting. Before serving, drizzle with chocolate syrup and top with peanuts, if desired.

Peanut Butter Frosting

Beat together 1 C. creamy peanut butter and ½ C. softened butter until light and fluffy. Gradually beat in 3½ C. powdered sugar and enough whipping cream to make desired spreading consistency (about ½ C.).

Amazing Amaretto

Ingredients

1 (15.25 oz.) box yellow cake mix

4 eggs

1 (5.1 oz.) box vanilla instant pudding mix

2 T. plus ½ C. amaretto liqueur, divided

½ C. vegetable oil

¼ tsp. almond extract or cherry flavoring

1 C. powdered sugar

Directions

1 Preheat oven to 350°. Grease and flour a 10″ Bundt pan.

2 In a large mixing bowl, beat together cake mix, eggs, pudding mix, 2 tablespoons amaretto, oil, almond extract, and ½ cup water until well blended. Spread batter in prepared pan and bake for 45 to 50 minutes or until cake tests done. Cool cake in pan for 10 minutes, then turn out onto a wire rack set over a rimmed baking sheet.

3 With a fork, poke holes in warm cake, about 1″ apart.

4 In a small bowl, stir together powdered sugar and remaining ½ cup amaretto until smooth. Slowly pour mixture over cake, allowing it to fill holes. Let cool for 2 hours. Sprinkle with additional powdered sugar before serving, if desired.

S'more Pokes

Ingredients

1 (15.25 oz.) box milk chocolate cake mix

Eggs, oil, and water as directed on cake mix box

1 (10 oz.) bag mini marshmallows

½ C. milk

1 T. lemon juice

½ tsp. vanilla extract

Cola Icing *(recipe follows)*

1 (8 oz.) tub whipped topping, thawed

Graham crackers, coarsely crumbled

Directions

1 Follow directions on cake mix box to prepare and bake a 9 x 13″ cake. Let cool for 15 minutes.

2 With the handle of a wooden spoon, poke holes in warm cake, about ½″ apart.

3 In a small saucepan over low heat, heat marshmallows and milk until melted and smooth, stirring constantly. Remove from heat and stir in lemon juice and vanilla. Pour marshmallow topping evenly over cake, allowing it to fill holes and coat cake. Cover and refrigerate for 2 hours.

4 Before serving, drizzle slightly cooled Cola Icing over cake; top with whipped topping and cracker crumbles. Garnish with chunks of milk chocolate candy and/or mini marshmallows, if desired.

Cola Icing

In a saucepan over medium heat, combine ¼ C. butter, 1½ T. unsweetened cocoa powder and 3½ T. cola (or root beer or water). Bring to a boil, stirring constantly. Remove from heat and whisk in 1¾ C. plus 2 T. powdered sugar and ½ tsp. vanilla extract until smooth.

Triple Strawberry

Ingredients

1 (16.25 oz.) box white cake mix

Egg whites, oil, and water as directed on cake mix box

1 (6 oz.) box strawberry gelatin

1 (12 oz.) bottle strawberry soda

Vanilla Topping *(recipe follows)*

Directions

1 Follow directions on cake mix box to prepare and bake a 9 x 13″ cake. Let cool for 15 minutes.

2 With a fork, poke holes in warm cake at ½″ intervals.

3 Combine gelatin with 1½ cups boiling water and stir until completely dissolved; let cool slightly. Stir in soda. Pour mixture slowly over cake, allowing it to fill holes. Refrigerate for 3 hours.

4 Frost cake with Vanilla Topping and chill for several hours. Top with sliced strawberries before serving, if desired.

Vanilla Topping

Whisk together 1 (5.1 oz.) box vanilla instant pudding mix and 1½ C. milk until smooth and thickened. Fold in 1 (8 oz.) tub thawed whipped topping.

So-Nice Spice

Ingredients

1 (15.25 oz.) box spice
cake mix

Eggs, oil, and water
as directed on cake
mix box

1 C. brown sugar

½ C. butter

Directions

1 Grease and flour two 5 x 9" loaf pans.

2 Follow directions on cake mix box to prepare cake
batter. Divide batter evenly among prepared pans and
bake for 25 to 30 minutes or until cakes test done. Run
a knife around sides of pans to loosen cakes.

3 In a medium saucepan over medium heat, melt
together brown sugar, butter, and ⅓ cup water, stirring
until blended.

4 With a fork, poke holes in hot cakes at ½" intervals.

5 Slowly pour brown sugar mixture over cakes, allowing
it to fill holes. Refrigerate for 1 to 2 hours. Serve with
ice cream and sprinkle with nutmeg, if desired.

note Can be made in a
9 x 13" pan, too.

Index

cakes

frostings